MERMAIDS

MERMAIDS

Beatrice Phillpotts

Ballantine Books · New York

First published in Great Britain 1980

Mermaids text © Beatrice Phillpotts 1980

Published in the United States by Ballantine Books, a division of Random House, Inc., New York, and simultaneously in Canada by Ballantine Books of Canada, Ltd., Toronto, Canada.

Library of Congress Cataloging in Publication Data

Phillpotts, Beatrice
  Mermaids

  Includes bibliographical references and index
  1. Mermaids. I. Title.
GR910.P44   398'.45   79-25838
ISBN 0-345-28657-X
ISBN 0-345-28656-1 (pb)

First Ballantine Books edition, hardcover and paperback: May 1980

Produced by: Russell Ash
            11 Wilmington House
            Highbury Crescent
            London N5 1RU
            England

Designed by Jonathan Gill-Skelton
Typesetting by Tameside Filmsetting Ltd.
Printed by Dai Nippon Printing Co. Ltd., Japan

Frontispiece: Daniel Maclise, *The Origin of the Harp*, c.1842

Contents

Acknowledgements

Among the many people who have helped in various ways with the book, I would like to extend special thanks to Rebecca John for her assistance with the picture research, Patricia Reed, Patrick Bade and Andrew Acquier for their continual interest and helpful suggestions, and most important, my editor and publisher Russell Ash, who has been an energetic and stimulating working companion throughout.

MERMAIDS

Supremely glamorous, forever combing her hair, just beyond reach, the elusively desirable mermaid offers the adventurous the challenge of the unknown and promise of wild, forbidden pleasures. Behind this seductive image, however, the 'sea enchantress' lurks as a symbol of death. Enticed by her voluptuous promises, generations of the unwary have been lured to their certain doom in a thousand different stories, the basis of a powerful and enduring sea-myth that still exerts a lingering credibility. A proliferation of mermaid sightings throughout the ages testifies to the continued eagerness to believe in one of the most attractive and compelling legendary beings.

The First Mermaids

Today's popular mermaid claims a long and distinguished ancestry dating back to the fish-tailed gods and goddesses worshipped by some of the earliest recorded civilizations. The ocean, as womb of creation and source of unfathomable wisdom has always played an important role in world beliefs, particularly among maritime nations.

Arnold Böcklin, *Calm Sea*, c.1886. Spurned by his lover, a sea-monster glides impotently away. The mermaid as *femme fatale* enjoyed a vogue in much late nineteenth-century art.

Its deities are among the most powerful in history and their strength lives on in the continued evolution of a host of submarine beings symbolic of the shifting dual nature of the sea as both life-giver and destroyer, to the mermaid, the fish-tailed seductress of folk belief who has dominated Western sea mythology since the early Christian era.

The earliest recorded ancestor of the mermaid was in fact a male sea god, Oannes, the 'great fish of the ocean', worshipped by the Babylonians in Accad around 5,000 BC. The Babylonians believed that the sea was the origin of all life and Oannes was therefore a supreme god. Like the sun, he rose from the waves in the morning and disappeared into the sea again at night and was a source of light and life to his people whom he instructed in all branches of the arts and sciences. A civilizing force for the good, Oannes symbolized the positive values connected with the ocean, a tradition continued in the wise, benevolent characters of the kind old sea gods from Greek myth, Nereus and Proteus.

Berossus, a Chaldean priest of the third century BC, described Oannes as follows: 'The whole body of the animal was like that of a fish; and had under a fish's head another head, and also feet below, similar to those of a man, subjoined to the fish's tail.' (Isaac P. Cory,

Oannes blessing the fleet. Part of a sculpture dating from the eighth century BC, discovered in the ruins of the palace of Sargon II at Khorsabad by Paul Emile Botta and illustrated in his *Monument de Ninive*, 1849.

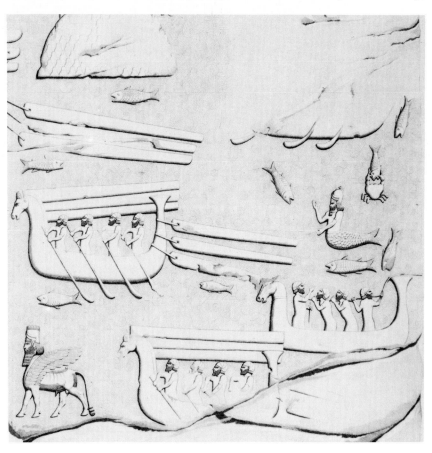

Odilon Redon, *Oannes*, c.1910. This amoeba-like Symbolist interpretation underlines Oannes' role as a universal life-force.

The Ancient Fragments, 1828). While early pictures accordingly showed him as a man draped in a fish cloak, this was later simplified to the half-man, half-fish form by which he became more popularly known.

Atargatis, a Semitic moon goddess worshipped by the Philistines, Syrians and Israelites provides the earliest female prototype for the mermaid. She was the feminine counterpart of the sun god Oannes, and an important fertility goddess who also personified the darker, night aspect of love as a potentially destructive force, an element integral to the mermaid legend.

Appropriately, Atargatis' own deification arose indirectly from an early fatal love affair involving a handsome young Syrian who fathered her illegitimate daughter, Semiramis. In a guilty fury, Atargatis murdered her lover, abandoned her baby and hurled herself into a nearby lake, from which she spectacularly re-emerged in fish form and was promptly deified. At first, like Oannes, she was represented as a mortal enveloped in a fish cloak, but this was later modified to a fish tail. The second-century AD Greek writer, Lucian, described a drawing he had come across in Phoenicia of Atargatis in her latter mermaid form: 'for in the upper half she is woman, but from the waist to the lower extremities runs in the tail of a fish.' (*De Sea Syria*, translated by William Tooke, 1820).

Atargatis will be better known today in her later guise as Aphrodite, Greek goddess of love, subsequently the Romans' Venus. Born from the sea in a scallop shell, Aphrodite retained Atargatis' close connections with the sea, but lost her fishy attributes. These were transferred instead to her marine escorts, the tritons, and their rarer female companions, the tritonids. Aphrodite was both a fertility figure, associated with marriage and family life, and the goddess of fair sailing, her constant companion the sacred dolphin, 'king of the fishes'. Many of the traditional attributes of Aphrodite/Venus were retained in the popular imagery of the mermaid legend but often employed towards different ends. The mermaid's mirror, included most often as a specific symbol of her vanity, was also a common feature associated with the goddess, but shown in conjunction with Venus, the mirror symbolized her planet in astrological tradition. The mermaid's comb, also a popular feature from scenes of Venus' toilette, carried additional sexual connotations which would have been immediately apparent to the Greeks and Romans, whose words for comb, *kteis* and *pecten*, also meant the female pudenda. An abundance of hair had traditionally signified an abundant love potential and Venus' flowing locks and concern with her coiffure, aspects continued in much mermaid imagery, served to provide a veiled reference to her role as fertility figure. The graceful attitudes suggested by the idea of Venus rising from the sea and drying her

Powerful symbols of procreation, fish deities were worshipped worldwide. In his first incarnation as a fish, Vishnu, second god of the Hindu trinity, saved mankind from the Flood and went on to found a new race. This illustration comes from *Tree of Paradise*, a seventeenth-century devotional text from Kashmir.

(Opposite) Clutching her magical mirror and comb, symbol of fertility and entanglement, a fifteenth-century siren gazes hungrily down from the fan-vaulted roof of Sherborne Abbey, Dorset.

Venus as fertility goddess with triton escort from a Romano-British mosaic dating from the early fourth century unearthed at Rudston, North Yorkshire. Flinging aside her mirror, Venus triumphantly brandishes the golden apple won in the celebrated Olympian beauty contest staged by Paris.

hair were an inspiration for many early writers and artists, among them the Greek poet Leonides of Tarentum from the third century BC who wrote:

> Just rising from her mother the sea, look,
> The Cyprian, whom Apelles has laboured to paint!
> How with her hand she takes hold of her tresses
> Damp from the sea! How she wrings out the foam
> From these wet locks of hers! Now Athene and Hera
> Will say, For beauty we no longer compete with you!

While the mermaid as an ideal beauty consecrated to the pursuit of love shares many temperamental affinities with the earlier love goddesses, particularly those emphasizing close links in passion between possession and destruction, visually, mermaid imagery is clearly much influenced by the frolicking sea nymphs of classical art. Many of the early naturalists such as Pliny the Elder and Plutarch described mermaids as nereids. 'And as for Meremaids called Nereides', wrote Pliny in his monumental *Historia Naturalis* (*c.* 80 AD), 'it is no fabulous tale that goeth of them: for looke how painters draw them, so they are indeed: onlie their bodie is rough and skaled all over, even in those parts wherein they resemble woman.' According to classical mythology, the nereids comprised the fifty daughters

of the sea god Nereus and his lovely wife, the 'grey-eyed' Doris, who together with her 2,999 sisters formed only part of the outsize marine family born of Oceanus' incestuous union with his sister Tethys, a dreadful case of in-breeding, but an eloquent testimony to the legendary fertility of the sea. Charming young women in shell head-dresses, the nereids were commonly portrayed riding hippocamps, marine hybrids, half-horse, half-dolphin. It was often difficult to tell in illustrations if the fish tails belonged to rider or mount, a potential confusion which no doubt prompted the subsequent transposition of mermaid and sea nymph.

Although lacking the fish-like attributes of their submarine sisters, the nereids did share certain other characteristics such as exquisite singing voices. While the mermaids employed this talent as a sinister weapon to ensnare passing sailors however, the amiable nereids reserved it for their father's entertainment. Indeed, far from harbouring any evil designs on sea travellers, the nereids set out to protect them as far as possible from the many dangers to be encountered on 'the great back of the sea'.

If the Greeks were hesitant to attach fish tails to their sea nymphs, they did possess a prototype merman in the shape of the sea god Triton, son of Poseidon, 'shaker of the earth', and his nereid wife Amphitrite. A group of minor sea deities, the tritons sprang up modelled on the original god, and a Greek travel writer of the second century AD, Pausanias, apparently personally acquainted with the species, provided the following detailed account of their appearance in his *Description of Greece*, translated by William Jones in 1918:

> On their heads they grow hair like that of the marsh frogs, not only in colour, but also in the impossibility of separating one hair from another. The rest of their body is rough with fine scales just as is the shark. Under their ears they have gills, and a man's nose, but the mouth is broader and the teeth are those of a beast. Their eyes seem to me blue, and they have hands, fingers and nails like the shells of the murex. Under the breast and belly is a tail like a dolphin's instead of feet.

Unlike the other classical sea gods such as Nereus and Proteus, who continued the Wise Old Man of the Sea tradition ultimately derived from Oannes, the tritons were a wilder, lustful race reputedly given to raping women and boys. One triton's habit of assaulting the women of Tanagra in Boeotia during their ritual ablutions before sacrificing to Dionysus, not unnaturally incurred the anger of the god. A fight ensued which the triton lost and he was driven away. Clearly the rampant nature of the fish-tailed triton was inherited by the merman, for the seventeenth-century writer John Swan related a similar story concerning the impact of a marauding merman on a coastal community. Following the abduction of one female resident

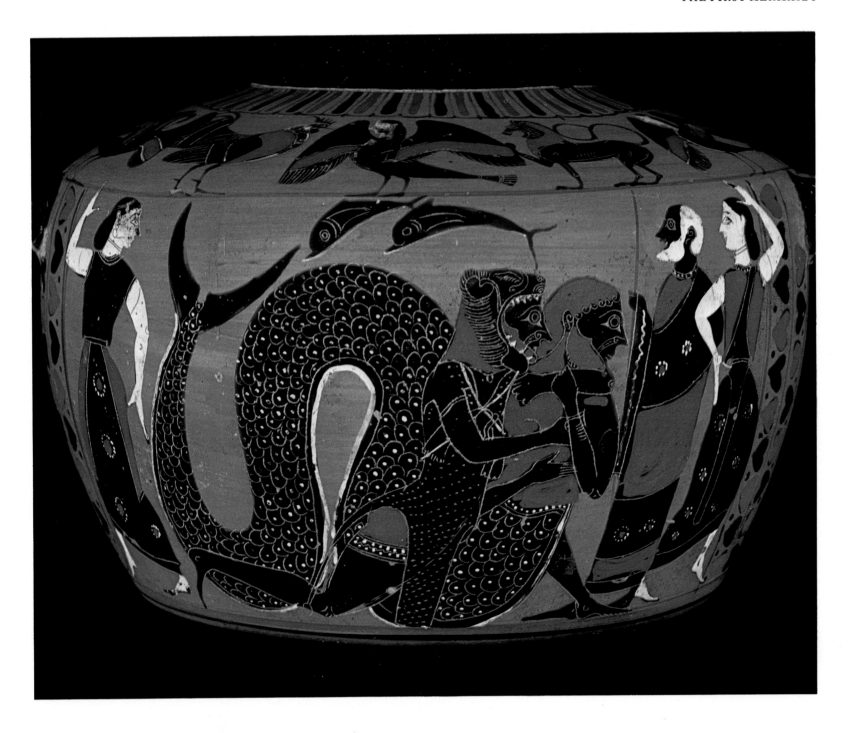

Heracles wrestles with the river god Achelous to win Deinara in this scene from a Greek red-figure vase.

A mermaid of the superior winged variety flaunts herself before an inferior twin-tailed sister amid a crowd of assorted oddities. An illustration from the *Buch der Natur*, 1475.

who had caught his fancy, the local citizens were forced to retaliate by banning solitary bathing, passing a new law 'that no woman should adventure to come near the sea, except her husband was with her.' (*Speculum Mundi*, 1635). Such stories, which represented the ocean in a distinctly threatening light as a cradle of evil monsters, continued a tradition stemming from the great navigational epics such as Odysseus' adventures which had earlier dramatically mythologized the horrors of the deep. These tales originally served

An elegantly coiffured, well-armoured *femme fatale* casually feeds a male victim to the fishes while debating on a suitable end for a second trapped admirer in Gustav Adolf Mossa's *La Nereide*, 1906.

an additional purpose as effective propaganda aids in promoting a fearful image of the sea which the Greeks as colonizing seafarers could use to discourage commercial rivals. The evil aspects of the mer-folk can be attributed in many ways to the formation of such attitudes.

If the tritons provided an early prototype for the merman, it was the Greek Sirens who influenced the mermaid character most pro-

Double danger on the high seas: saved from a shipwreck by the intervention of a mermaid, a king is forced to give her his first child as a reward. One of Henry Ford's illustrations to *The Brown Fairy Book* by Andrew Lang, 1904.

Pellegrino Tibaldi, *Poseidon punishing Odysseus*, 1554–5, a painted panel from the ceiling of the University, Bologna. Poseidon attempts to revenge himself on Odysseus for blinding his son.

foundly. Indeed the bird-woman Sirens were actually to metamorphose from bird to fish as they became more closely identified in the popular imagination with the fish-tailed mermaid. The bird form of the Sirens derived from the ancient Egyptian soul birds, the *Ba*. Like the *Ba*, the Sirens were primarily demons of death, souls sent to catch a soul, and as such often appeared as carvings on tombs, presumably as a guard to fend off their predatory sisters. Their bird shape and close connection with death was popularly explained in Classical mythology as their punishment for their failure as Proserpina's attendants to prevent her abduction to the Underworld. Perched on an island near the straits where the fearsome sea monsters, Scylla 'the gnawer' and Charybdis 'the swallower' reputedly lurked ready to pounce on unsuspecting crews, the Sirens surrounded themselves with the bleached bones of their victims ensnared by the fatal temptations of their song. Only two seafarers were alleged to have escaped their clutches, Odysseus, who took the precaution of lashing himself to the mast and stuffing the ears of his crew with beeswax, and Orpheus, who managed to out-play them on his legendary lyre.

Fatal seductresses, the Sirens as soul-birds enticing the living to join them in death were the direct ancestresses of the mermaids who traditionally lure men to their doom with their songs of forbidden delights. Homer's Sirens appealed to the weaknesses of the spirit, tempting Odysseus with the gift of supreme knowledge, a god-like attribute and therefore a fatal presumption on the part of a mere mortal. Plato described siren song as 'the music of the spheres', an irresistible celestial harmony which transcended human comprehension. Later the emphasis changed from spiritual to worldly

Harpies and hippocamps fight it out in one of Andrea Mantegna's dramatic engravings in his Battle of the Sea Gods cycle.

Triumphant marine processions from classical myth were a popular theme in Renaissance art. Raphael's *Triumph of Galatea*, c.1513, depicts the legendary sea beauty with a mixed entourage of marine escorts.

Gilbert Bayes' *Little Mermaid*, 1938. A decoration in salt-glazed stoneware by Doulton & Co on the St Pancras Housing Association estate, London.

temptation and the mermaid-siren moralized by the Medieval Church embodied the lure of fleshly pleasures to be feared and shunned by the God-fearing.

A frequent feature of the popular epic romances and natural history books, the mermaid gradually established herself as a distinct entity in the early Christian era. For Pliny the Elder, the fish-tailed women were a reality, living proof of nature's splendid diversity. There are several mermaid sightings in his *Historia Naturalis* and even an account of a remarkable mass monster tide which occurred in 'a certain Island upon the coast of the province of Lions' at the beginning of the first century AD. More than three hundred creatures were washed ashore 'of a wonderful varietie and bignesse, differing asunder' including sea-elephants, aquatic rams 'with teeth standing out, and horns also', together with 'many Meremaids'.

Tales of the heroic exploits of Alexander the Great were among the favourite reading of the period and encounters with strange varieties of submarine women often added additional spice to such adventures. Once travelling in the East beside a broad river where mussels reputedly grew 'so great that six men might make a meal of one', Alexander heard reports of giant women who lived in the water like fishes. Siren-like, these creatures would lure any men they saw 'into the water, if he knew not their craft'. Once in their clutches, escape was impossible; 'they bound him to great reeds and forced him to make sport for them till at last they killed him'. Nothing daunted by these dreadful rumours, Alexander and his men managed to capture two of these predatory mermaids who were 'as white as snow, their hair came down to their feet round their body, and they were taller than men have custom to be'. Unable to survive for long out of water, however, both died soon afterwards.

Mermaids were not confined solely to the more rarified regions of epic romance it appeared, but were a common feature of the marine life around the British Isles. Ireland even boasted her own sanctified mermaid, Liban, a young woman drowned in a great flood of 90 AD,

A doomed sailor drowns under the haughty gaze of his seductress. *The Siren*, a morbidly romantic subject painted with wistful relish by the High Victorian artist, John William Waterhouse.

A mermaid thwarted of her prey by the timely intervention of a flying gnome. One of William de Morgan's illustrations to his sister Mary's fairy story, *On a Pincushion*, 1877.

who had sprouted a salmon's tail and together with her pet dog (transformed into an otter) spent the next 500 years swimming around the Irish coast. Wearied eventually of her solitary submarine life-style, Liban implored the aid of a local saint, St Comgall. Divine assistance was successfully secured and an immediate passage to Heaven granted, where the blessed Liban was seated in glory 'among the holy virgins, and held in honour and reverence as God ordained'. (P. W. Joyce, *Old Celtic Romances*, 1894).

Prior to her heavenly ascent, Liban had spent several days somewhat ingloriously, splashing about in a boat half filled with water ogled by growing crowds, while St Comgall conducted his negotiations with God. The event was duly recorded in *The Annals of the Kingdom of Ireland* (558 AD). By 887 AD, however, such incidents had clearly become a commonplace for a gigantic mermaid measuring 195 feet and 'whiter than the swan all over' stranded that year rated no more than the most casual mention in the *Annals*. When Gervase of Tilbury, the historian and travel writer, remarked on the con-

Bartholomaeus Spranger's *Glaucus and Scylla*, c.1582. The painting celebrates the ill-fated love of the sea god for a nymph. Spurned by Scylla, Glaucus begged the enchantress Circe for a love-potion, but she spitefully changed his sweetheart into a hideous monster.

siderable number of mermaids and mermen living in the British sea in his *Otia Imperialia* (1212), he was clearly reporting a serious piece of folklore. Certainly St Patrick's alleged custom of banishing old pagan women from the earth by turning them into mermaids can only have aggravated the evident marine congestion.

A passing monk-fish steers a course through busy sea traffic while scholars discourse. From *Hortus Sanitatis*, 1491.

Seduction of the faithful: Noah looks on anxiously as fellow passengers on the Ark ogle nearby mermaids. A woodcut from the *Biblia Sacra Germanica*, known as the Nuremberg Bible, 1483.

Mermaids, Sex and Religion

Faced with the mass of accumulated stories and reported sightings relating to a patent sinner who nonetheless clearly commanded a large popular following, the Western Roman Church countered by enlisting the mermaid as a spectacular propaganda aid in the cause of religious duty. Moralized, she now existed solely as a siren eager to lure the upright citizen from the straight and narrow. The censorious Church attitude reflected a central repressive approach to sex in general. Writing to St Augustine in 601 AD, Pope Gregory had adopted a stern stand on the matter, declaring that 'Lawful

(Right) A merman and his mate, as spotted from the banks of the Nile by a strolling officer. One of many curious incidents described and illustrated in Aldrovandi's *Historia Monstrorum*, 1642. (Below) Mer-mother and child are joined by a pet monkey in this marginal decoration from a thirteenth-century manuscript.

A Romanesque mermaid rubs
shoulders with an angel on a
decorated capital at St Peter's,
Bologna.

intercourse should be for the procreation of offspring, and not for mere pleasure', and continuing:

> It is not fitting that a man who has approached his wife should enter Church before he has washed nor is he to enter at once though washed . . . for when a man's mind is attracted to those pleasures by lawless desire, he should not regard himself as fitted to join in Christian worship until these heated desires cool in the mind, and he has cease to labour under wrongful passions.
>
> (Bede, *A History of the English Church and People*, translated by Leo Sherley-Price, 1955).

Symbols of Vice, the voluptuous harlot-mermaids as represented by the medieval Church personified the lure of base, unnatural desires which stood between a man and his chance of salvation.

As a vivid reminder of banned pleasures, the mermaid enjoyed a revival of interest in the Middle Ages. Mermaid carving began to figure increasingly in church decoration and mermaid illustrations formed a popular feature of the bestiary books that enjoyed a great vogue between the eleventh and fourteenth centuries, in which fantastic descriptions of real and imaginary creatures were used to illustrate points of Christian dogma. As fatal charmer, the mermaid continued the siren tradition but in fish rather than bird form. The snaky sinuosities of her tail made the mermaid form a particular favourite in Church carvings which could also neatly and decoratively point a moral lesson, and soon an army of shapely sirens carved on the capitals of the pillars and pew ends winked and leered at the assembled faithful.

(Right) Carved mermaid bench ends from Ripon Minster, Yorkshire, c.1490, and (above) Crowcombe church, Somerset, c.1534.

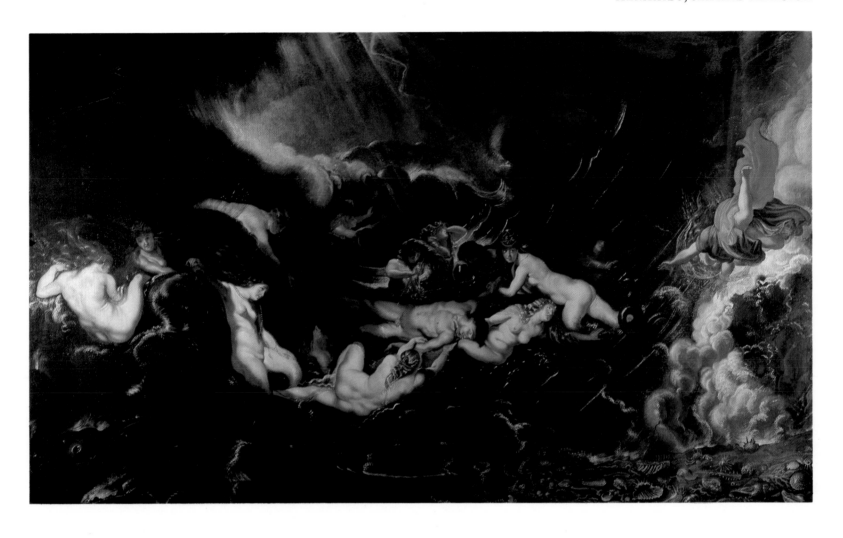

Rubens' *Hero and Leander*, c.1607. Hero throws herself into the sea to join her drowned lover as mermaids lament.

Confronted by a fleet of predatory mermaids brandishing their fearsome fish trophies, symbols of the abducted Christian soul, the medieval churchgoer was urged to reflect on the righteousness of his own life-style. Some church authorities, quite understandably, feared for the spiritual benefit of such possible musings. St Bernard of Clairvaux forcibly expressed his own anxiety for the spiritual welfare of his monks surrounded by such salacious beauties:

> Again in the cloisters what is the meaning of these ridiculous monsters, of that deformed beauty, that beautiful deformity before the very eye of the brethren when reading? Such endless forms appear everywhere, that it is more pleasant to read in the stonework than in the books, and to spend the day admiring these oddities than in meditating on the law of God.

The transition from bird to fish form was more gradual in contemporary literature, as traced through the illustrated bestiaries of the period. The earliest mention of a fish-tailed siren appears in *Liber Monstrorum*, written around the turn of the eighth century, which stated: 'From the head to the navel they are women in shape: below, they have scaley fishes' tails which they hide in the flood'. This image was not firmly established for several hundred years however. Hesitant to commit themselves absolutely, many writers arrived at bizarre compromises. Thus, for Philippe de Thaon writing in the twelfth century, the siren was a woman to the waist 'having falcon's

(Above) A fourteenth-century wall painting from Vamlingbo, Sweden. (Below) Feathered and finned mermaids bear down on their sleeping prey in an early fourteenth-century drawing.

Armand Point's *The Siren*, 1897. A Symbolist interpretation of the legend of Odysseus and the Sirens.

feet and the tail of a fish'. Guillaume Le Clerc, writing in the following century, claimed that the siren could be either a fish or a bird-woman, while his contemporary, Pierre de Beauvais, assured his readers that although two of the sirens were part fish, the third was part bird.

If the form of the siren tended to waver disconcertingly in such learned texts between bird and fish, the overall message remained quite clear: as Bartholmaeus Anglicus grimly inveighed in *De Proprietatibus Rerum* (*c.* 1470), the sirens were 'strong whores that drew men that passed by to poverty and mischief'. The popular story of Odysseus and the Sirens served as a powerful moral allegory of the manifold temptations of the flesh. 'Let not a woman with a flowing train cheat you of your senses', thundered Clement of Alexandria in his *Exhortation to the Heathen*, 'sail past the song; it works death; exert your will, and you have overcome ruin; bound to the wood of the Cross, you shall be freed from destruction. The Word of God will be your pilot, and the Holy Spirit will bring you to anchor in the haven of Heaven.'

Odysseus and the Sirens on a fifth-century BC Attic vase.

Herbert Draper's *Ulysses and the Sirens*, c.1909. Lashed to the mast, with his crew's ears stuffed with beeswax, Ulysses (Odysseus) outwits the Sirens.

Alongside such carefree rapacious sirens, ever-eager to rob a man of his chances of immortality, there existed a smaller group of more highly principled mermaids who, anxious for salvation spurned their own baser natures. Celtic mythology supplied the edifying example of the blessed Liban and also recorded the poignant story of the less resolute Mermaid of Iona who was unable to relinquish her ocean home for her promised soul and whose bitter tears reputedly formed themselves into the greenish-grey pebbles peculiar to the island's shore. The influence of the Church was also apparent in the many recorded attempts to convert stranded mermaids. Accordingly, a mermaid washed ashore in fifteenth-century Holland had her spiritual as well as her physical wants attended to as a matter of course. Once she had been fed and cleansed of the 'sea-mosse, which did stick about her', this mermaid was taken to Haarlem 'where she would obey her mistris, and (as she was taught) kneel down with her before the crucifix'. (John Swan, *Speculum Mundi*, 1635). The medieval theory that the sea contained the counterpart of every creature living on land as the original womb of all things, also engendered a belief in a submarine religious hierarchy of mer-folk, presumably on hand ready to minister to those anxious to rectify their 'fallen' state. In 1531, according to the British clergyman, John Gregory, in his

The sea-monk and sea-bishop, submarine ecclesiastics from Aldrovandi's *Historia Monstrorum*, 1642.

Jacques de Gheyn II's *Poseidon and Amphitrite*, 1792. Poseidon, the Greek lord of the sea, married the nereid Amphitrite and fathered the merman Triton.

Opuscula (1650), one such divine was captured in Poland, representing 'the whole appearance and appointments of a Bishop. This Sea-Monster was brought to the King, and after a while seemed very much to express to him, that his minde was to return to his own Element again'. Fortunately the King was of the same opinion, feeling perhaps that there were more converts to be made underwater, and the Bishop 'was carried back to the Sea, and cast himself into it immediately'.

Mermaid Marriages

One means of gaining a soul, according to popular tradition, was marriage with a mortal. In the view of the sixteenth-century scholar Paracelsus, the underwater spirits or 'undines' were endowed with the same mental gifts as mankind, and equal in all other respects save for their lack of a soul, which could however be obtained through marriage with a mortal. This theory was the genesis of the popular nineteenth-century romance, *Undine* by de la Motte Fouqué, which dealt with the unhappy consequences of such a mixed marriage. An earlier model for the water spirit Undine was the legendary French beauty Melusina, the mermaid who won the heart of Raymond, Count of Poitiers, and married him on condition that she spend every Saturday in complete privacy. Neglectful of this promise, Raymond was subsequently treated to the alarming spectacle of:

> Melusyne within the bathe unto her navell, in fourme of a woman kymbying her heere, and from the navell downward in lyknes of a grete serpent, the tayll as great & thykk as a barell, and so long it was she made it to touch oftymes, while raymondyn beheld her, the rouf of the chambre that was ryght hye.
> (Jean D'Arras, *Melusine*, an 1895 facsimile of a sixteenth-century translation, edited by A. K. Donald).

Unable to adjust himself to his wife's shocking secret, Raymond later rounded on his spouse in a moment of stress, calling her 'an odious

Assorted fishy hybrids, from *Uraltes Chymisches Werk* by Abraham Eleazar, 1760.

Submarine courtship from an
illustrated songsheet of the
1860s.

(Above) The dangers of spying on one's wife: Raymond's discovery that he has unwittingly married a monster, shown on the titlepage of *Melusine* by Jean d'Arras, 1530. (Right) The water nymph Undine's wedding day, an illustration from *Undine, A Legend*, by the Baron de la Motte Fouqué, 1885.

serpent', whereupon she, quite understandably, instantly vanished.

The intriguing possibilities of a mixed mermaid marriage provided a staple of folk legend. On the whole it seemed that mermaids made excellent and conscientious wives, being good cooks and prolific mothers. First it was necessary to catch one's mer-wife, however, a tricky business involving the wily removal of some vital part of her sea-going equipment, such as her magic cap, belt or comb. Woe

Trapped by a lamia: *The Kiss of the Enchantress* by Isobel Gloag, c.1890.

A mer-wife rejoins her under-water brood. One of Ludwig Richter's illustrations to Rüfaus' *Volksmärchen der Deutchen*, 1917.

(Right) Exposed as a water nymph, Undine returns to her native element. An illustration by Arthur Rackham to a 1909 edition of *Undine*.

betide any husband who failed to hide them away securely enough for subsequent repossession unfailingly signalled irretrievable marital breakdown as, cheerfully shrugging off the weight of family responsibilities the oblivious merwives plunged back into the sea. One Scottish folklore character, Johnny Croy, wisely safeguarded himself against such an eventuality by contracting a seven year marriage with the proviso that at its termination he would leave with his wife. Forfeiting only one of his seven children, whom granny

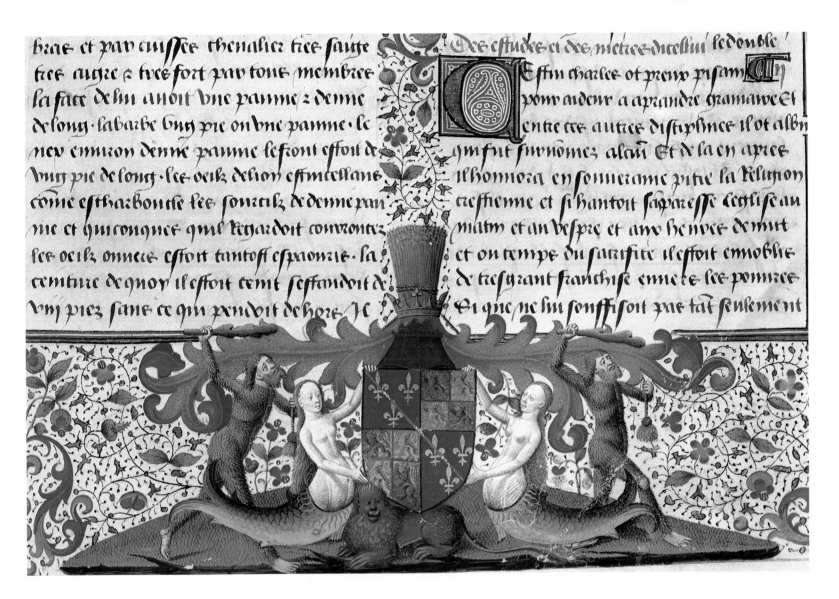

Mermaids became a favourite heraldic emblem. Here they mingle with wild men in this fifteenth-century coat-of-arms belonging to Jacques d'Armagnac.

Croy had taken the precaution of branding with the cross, he 'his braw young wife and their six bairn' set sail together for a new life at the end of the seven years.

So persuasive were these stories that many families claimed mer-descent. One family recorded living in the parish of Fern, Easter Ross in the Hebrides at the end of the nineteenth century numbered a merman, cunningly deprived of his magic belt, among their ancestors. In Europe the mermaid Melusina naturally appears in the heraldic arms of the House of Lusignan in memory of Raymond's own ill-fated marriage. Such was the glamorous Melusina's fame that the Houses of Luxembourg, Rohan and Sassenaye all altered their pedigrees to claim mer-descent.

Sea Sightings

It is the elusive, single mermaid who has traditionally exercised the strongest lure, and none more so than the mermaid spotted after weeks of sea travel spent out of female company. The steady stream of mermaid sightings reported since Pliny the Elder originally lent his support to the phenomenon in the first century AD, received an additional boost in the great era of maritime expansion of the sixteenth and seventeenth centuries. While many such reports can be discounted as sailors' yarns, the unsensationalized graphic account of a sighted mermaid in the explorer Henry Hudson's log does carry a certain quiet conviction. On the morning of 13 June 1608, two

A popular design feature of many early maps, these mermaids come from the Hondius map of Africa, 1631.

The 'sea maid' from Shakespeare's *A Mid-summer Night's Dream*, illustrated by Arthur Rackham in 1908.

(Above) A fish-wife in every sense of the word. (Right) Crushed in a pythonesque embrace, another victim meets a watery end in this *fin-de-siècle* engraving.

months out of port en route to discover a new passage to the East Indies, he recorded that:

> one of our companie looking over boord saw a Mermaid . . . From the Navill upward, her backe and breasts were like a womans (as they say that saw her) her body as big as one of us: her skin very white; and long hair hanging downe behinde, of colour blacke; in her going down they saw her tayle which was like the tayle of a Porposse, and speckled like a Macrell. Their names that saw her were Thomas Hilles and Robert Raynar.

The discovery of new countries brought an influx of reports of fresh zoological marvels among which varieties of mermaid frequently featured. *A Treatise of Brasil*, 'written by a Portugall' in 1601, served as an excuse to perpetuate some of the more colourful aspects of the myth. The local genus describe in the treatise was, it appeared, a particularly rapacious variety; indeed so fearful were the Brazilians of the mermen 'that many die onely with the thought of them'. The beautiful long-haired mermaids were no less ferocious and delighted in pythonesque embraces, kissing and grasping their victims so hard 'that they crush it in pieces remaining whole'. Finicky eaters, these *femmes fatales* sampled 'onely the eies, the nose, the points of the fingers and toes, and privie members', discarding

(Above) Edvard Munch's *The Lady from the Sea* (detail), 1896. The siren held a fascination for Munch who equated sex with loss of identity and death. (Below) A sea-demon from Aldrovandi's *Historia Monstrorum*, 1642.

Oberon and Puck listen to the mermaid's song in one of Robert Anning Bell's illustrations to *A Midsummer Night's Dream*, 1895.

the remainder as awful warnings along the local beaches. Some sea travellers refused to indulge the public taste for distant marvels however. Captain Uring, in the foreword to his *Voyages and Travels* (1726), bluntly expressed his own aversion to such sensation-seeking, denouncing the 'many Sea-Voyages and Travels lately published by Persons unknown, which are all made Stories, on purpose to impose on the World and get Money'.

If actual belief was on the decline by the eighteenth century, interest remained unflagging bolstered by the continued reports of mermaid sightings from around the world. A remarkable occurrence in Denmark in 1723 must have converted many of the sceptics, when a Royal Commission set up specifically to investigate the phenomenon and, it was hoped, to banish such idle speculation once and for all, allegedly found itself face-to-face with a palpable merman. By

Albrecht Dürer's *The Rape of Amymone*, c.1500. In Greek myth one of King Danaus' fifty daughters, Amymone, was abducted by Poseidon. His turtleshell shield symbolizes the fertility of the waters.

A merman, sea-monkey and sea-Turk, some of the many natural curiosities described and illustrated in *Hortus Sanitatis*, 1491.

some happy chance the creature in question surfaced just beside the Royal Commission boat on a fact-finding tour of the Faeroes. Any existing doubts were immediately dispelled and the members of the Commission were even able to report back that this merman had deep-set eyes and a long black beard which looked as if it had been cut.

From the Far East came many reports of mer-creatures sighted off the Moluccas. One particularly splendid specimen known as the Mermaids of Amboine was reputedly captured and kept in a tank for several days but refusing all food soon died. She appeared in *Poissons écrevisses et crabes de diverse couleurs et figures extraordinaires, que l'on trouve autour des Isles Moluques*, a magnificently illustrated natural history book which was published in Amsterdam in 1717. With her olive colouring and vivid pink, orange and blue markings she must rank as one of the most exotic mermaids ever recorded. Peter the Great of Russia, much struck with her tropical beauty, wrote to the publisher requesting further information, and a local authority, François Valentijn, former superintendent of the churches in the colonies, was called upon to supply more facts. Unfortunately he was unable to corroborate the existence of the Amboine mermaid whom he had not seen but did send a detailed description of a merman recently viewed at close quarters. Bluish-grey and sporting a mossy fisherman's cap, this creature was evidently of a fearful disposition and dived for cover as soon as it was conscious of being watched.

Historical Hoaxes

Hitherto the public had relied mainly on second-hand reports to confirm the existence of mermaids, but the late eighteenth century saw the beginning of a craze for stuffed mermaids which promised closer experience of the phenomenon. Mermaid exhibitions were

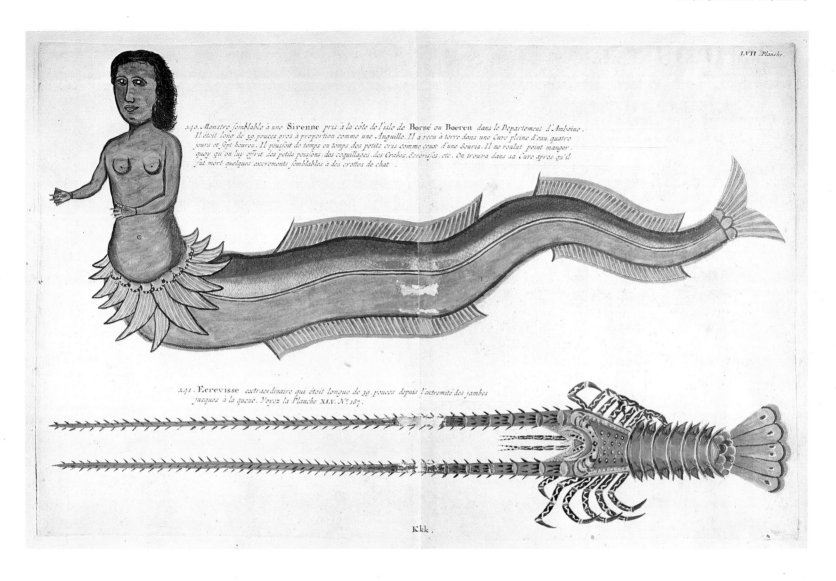

The Mermaid of Amboine, 'drawn from the life'. One of the splendid hand-tinted plates to *Poissons, écrevisses et crabes de diverse couleurs et figures extraordinaires, que l'on trouve autour des Isles Moluques*, 1717.

The 'Fejee Mermaid' (*Sunday Herald*, 17 July 1842).

nothing new. The travel writer, Samuel Purchas in his *Pilgrimes* (1625) included a reference to a mermaid 'skinne' on show in 1565 at Thora, a busy port on the Red Sea, but it was not until the eighteenth century that the business really got under way. The attractive creatures depicted sporting on the handbills were a far cry from the hideous hybrids actually on display, a disconcerting proportion of which were rapidly exposed as fakes. Dr James Parsons' 'surprizing young Mermaid, taken on the coast of Acapulco' and exhibited at Charing Cross in London in the eighteenth century, was in reality a malformed foetus, while the famous East Indian mermaid, first shown in London at the Turf Coffee House, St James's, was dourly described by one visitor, Mr J. Murray of Camarthen, as the unsightly combination of the 'upper part of the long-armed ape attached to the tail portion of the genus *Salmo*'. The monkey and fish combination clearly provided a favourite format but was a miserable approximation to the enticing beauties of marine legend. As the naturalist George Johnstone aptly remarked in 'The tests by which a real mermaid may be discovered' (*Magazine of Natural History*, 1829): 'I

BY THE KING'S ROYAL AUTHORITY.

WHEREAS many have IMAGINED that the HISTORY of

Mermaids,

mentioned by the Authors of Voyages, is fabulous, and only introduced as the *Tale of a Traveller*; there is now in Town an Opportunity, for the Nobility, Gentry, &c. to have an occular Demonstration of its Reality.

This curious and surprising Nymph, even the Queen of the Sea-Fishes, was taken in the Year 1784, in the Gulph of Stanchio, on Board of a Merchant-Man called *the Good Luck*, Captain Fortier. It is exactly three Feet in Length, and in Form like a Woman from the Head down to the lower Part of the Waist, and half a Fish from thence downwards, and is as perfect at this very Moment as when alive, standing in the same Position as when it rises at Sea, between Wind and Water, in order to make resound the neighbouring Echoes of the Archipelago with her sweet and melodious Voice.

(Right) Mermaids in bondage: two sultry hybrids from a seventeenth-century engraving.

(Opposite) A 'curious and surprising Nymph . . . taken in the Year 1784, in the Gulph of Stanchio', and exhibited at the Great Room, Spring Gardens, London, in 1795.

(Above) Sizing up a possible mermaid exhibit: an illustration to *The Life of P.T. Barnum Written by Himself*, 1855. (Right) A 300 year old stuffed 'mermaid' on view at the 1961 British Museum exhibition, *Fakes and Forgeries*.

cannot help thinking that in such cases we are not less deceived than our ancestors were, though it may be less agreeably; for their mermaids sang, and combed their sunny locks, and were, besides, extremely personable monsters, while ours are not only altogether mute, but as ugly as can well be conceived.'

During the height of the craze large financial profits were to be made from the spectacle, as demonstrated by the successes of the famous nineteenth-century entrepreneur and showman, Phineas T. Barnum. Barnum's highly lucrative 'Fejee Mermaid' owed her popularity to a skilful advance publicity campaign which built up sufficient interest for an exhibition to be mounted at the Concert Hall

The 'Fejee Mermaid' hits Broadway: one of Barnum's advertisements for the American Museum exhibition in 1842.

AMERICAN
MUSEUM & GARDENS!
Corner of Broadway and Ann-street,
Under the Management of Mr. P. T. Barnum.
WONDER OF THE WORLD!!
FOR ONE WEEK MORE!!!

Every Day & Evening this week, commencing on Monday August 22.

☞The Manager being ever desirous to gratify his

Numerous Patrons!

And determined to spare no exertions which may result in securing every

Wonderful Novelty!

Has in accordance with

☞ Universal Desire! ☟

Effected an engagement for a short time longer with the Proprietor of the most wonderful curiosity ever discovery, the

REAL
MERMAID!

Which was exhibited during the past week at Concert Hall, in Broadway, and which elicited the wonder and amazement of Hundreds of

NATURALISTS

And other Scientific Persons

Whose doubts regarding the existance of such an

EXTRAORDINARY CREATION

Have been entirely removed

The exhibition of the MERMAID will CLOSE every evening, at 9 o'clock.

No Extra Charge

Will be made for Admission to the Museum.

In order to accommodate the vast crowds of Ladies and Gentlemen, which visit this Establishment, Day Visitors will not be admitted Free in the Evening this week but there will be a

Day Performance Every Afternoon

Commencing at 4 o'clock. The Performances in the afternoon will be precisely the same as those in the evening.

S.H. Sime's drawing, *The Mermaid*, which was published in the periodical, *Eureka* in 1897.

on Broadway 'positively for one week only!' in the summer of 1842. So popular was the mermaid, whom Barnum privately described as 'an ugly dried-up, black-looking, and diminutive specimen' (*The Life of P. T. Barnum Written by Himself*, 1855) that she was subsequently transferred to the American Museum in New York where she almost tripled the Museum's takings in the first month.

In fact the 'Fejee Mermaid' was none other than the East Indian mermaid previously exhibited at St James's in 1822 and surely one of the most well-exposed specimens in the history of the trade.

Gustav Klimt's *Sea Serpents I*, 1904.
An erotic embrace amid a richly
abstracted submarine setting.

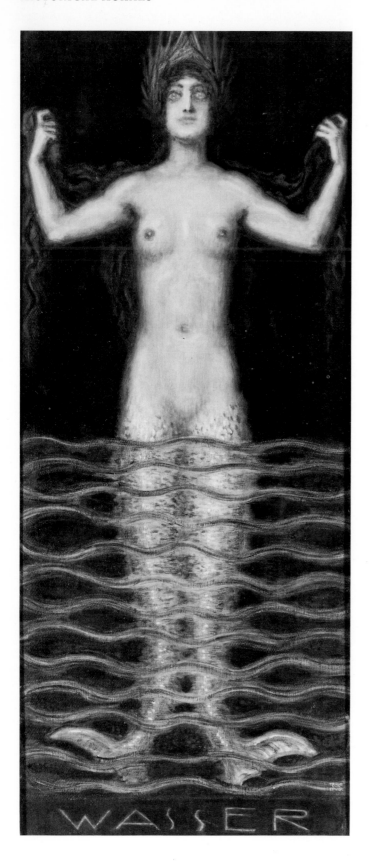

WASSER

Reputed to have been netted by a north Chinese fisherman, she had been purchased for $5,000 by a Captain Eades in Java. Eades had great confidence in his mermaid, an implicit faith not shared by the experts to whom he submitted her for examination on his arrival in London. William Clift, curator of the Hunterian Museum, Glasgow, declared the mermaid to be nothing more than a 'palpable imposition', the ingenious combination of an orang-outang and a salmon, an opinion later echoed by the sceptical Mr Murray. Nothing daunted, Captain Eades proceeded to display his mermaid in St James's where she proved a great attraction, drawing from three to four hundred people daily and providing an eloquent testimony to the continued credibility of the mermaid myth.

Stuffed mermaids continue to attract considerable interest as demonstrated by the exhibition of fakes and frauds held by the British Museum in 1961 in which two embalmed 'mermaids' believed to date from the seventeenth century featured among the exhibits. While one followed the traditional monkey/fish format favoured by the perpetrators of the 'Fejee Mermaid' among others, the second exhibit with her large glass eyes, gleaming ivory teeth and arched tail presented a more imaginative, if still basically unalluring appearance. The development of X-ray photography however necessitated a degree of sophistication in hoaxing singularly lacking in this early glass-eyed charmer, revealing a complex inner network of wires that did little to support her credibility.

It is impossible now to tell how many alleged sightings were hoaxes perpetrated on a gullible public and passed down as fact, but one such colourful episode was clearly revealed as a deliberate fraud. The unlikely perpetrator of this particular mermaid hoax was Robert Stephen Hawker, later to become vicar of Morwenstow in Cornwall, whose elaborate student stunt lasting several moonlit nights attracted considerable crowds to the Bude coast in the summer of 1825 or 1826, according to his Victorian biographer, Sabine Baring Gould. 'Seated on a rock some distance from the shore, wearing a plaited seaweed wig which hung in lank streamers half way down his back, [Hawker] enveloped his legs in an oilskin wrap, and otherwise naked sat on the rock, flashing the moon beams about from a hand mirror, and sang and screamed till attention was arrested.' Understandable discomfort and hoarseness eventually forced the abandonment of the stunt and with a loud 'God Save the King', Hawker plunged into the waves never to be seen in mermaid form again. A modern biographer, Piers Brendon, was more sceptical of the credulity of the local inhabitants, claiming the incident ended abruptly when an angry farmer loudly threatened the apparition with a peppering of buckshot.

(Above) A seventeenth-century mermaid carved onto an oak bread-oven door. (Opposite) Franz von Stuck's *Water*, c.1913. A design for one of the four elements (earth, fire, air and water) incorporated as decorative reliefs at the Villa Stuck, Munich.

Folk Heroine and Creative Muse

The persistence of the mermaid myth in Europe undoubtedly owed much to the nineteenth-century revival of interest in the national folk heritage which stimulated the systematic recording and preservation of legends from regional cultural tradition. *Grimm's Fairy Tales* (1812), a collection of traditional stories then still being told in Hesse, was one such early compilation and its popularity inspired a spate of similar literary efforts all over Europe. Through these books, the general reader was introduced to novel ramifications of the mermaid legend and the varied character traits of her supernatural kin lurking in seas and inland waters all over the world.

In his early folk survey, *Fairy Mythology* (1850), Thomas Keightley investigated the submarine *femmes fatales* of European legend. The *morgens* of Brittany it appeared were related to the evil enchantress of Arthurian legend, Morgan Le Fay, and lured all those who ventured too near irrevocably down into their gold and crystal underwater palaces. Lorelei, siren of the Rhine, amused herself in traditional style in enticing passing sailors onto the rocks, while any glimpse of the delectable Norwegian *Havfrue* about her daily business, 'when a thin mist hangs over the sea, sitting on the surface of the water,

Charles Shannon's *The Fisherman and the Mermaid*, c.1902, the painting on which Shannon based his illustration to Oscar Wilde's *A House of Pomegranates*, 1891.

'Full fathom five', one of Edmund Dulac's illustrations to Shakespeare's *The Tempest*, 1908.

and combing her long golden hair with a golden comb, or driving up her snow-white cattle to feed on the strands and small islands', portended iminent disaster, as all local fishermen knew to their cost.

The male of the species according to Keightley was no less predatory. The German *nix*, though handicapped by green teeth, nonetheless frequently succeeded in luring attractive young women down into his submarine love-nest, and many stories recount of mortal mid-wives being called in to assist at subsequent births. Like the equally unprepossessing Irish *merrow*, endowed with mossy teeth, green hair, a red nose and pig's eyes, the *nix* also indulged in the antisocial pursuit of trapping drowned sailors' souls under lobster pots, thus effectively ruining their owners' chances of salvation. The Scandinavian *neck* cut a more dashing figure, with his golden curls and musical talents, but his custom of disciplining 'any haughty maiden who makes an ill return to the love of her wooer' was not entirely altruistic.

Such local legends could be used to the advantage of the ingenious as illustrated by the shrewd example of a fourteenth-century ruler, King Chen, as recorded in West African legend. When the onset of paralysis in his legs threatened the credibility of his symbolic role as the healthy and vigorous life force of his people, thus automatically signalling his own death, Chen announced that his legs had turned to mud fish, thus proving that he was the incarnation of the sea god

Scenes from a happy mer-childhood: two of William Heath Robinson's illustrations for 'The Little Mermaid' in *Hans Andersen's Fairy Tales*, 1913.

Herbert Draper's *Water Baby*, 1890.

Charles Ricketts' illustrations to 'The Fisherman and his Soul' from *A House of Pomegranates*, 1891.

Olokun. The ruse was successful, and saved from ever revealing the true cause of his immobility, King Chen continued his reign in even greater glory. Clearly belief in such sea legends died hard in West Africa for a case of mermaid deception was reported in Accra as recently as 1956, involving a gullible cashier who robbed his office of £516 as a result of a beach encounter with a 'mermaid' who had promised to double the money for a modest £16 commission.

The nineteenth-century folk revival inspired the creation of a spate of hybrid *femmes fatales* who haunted the literary and artistic imagination of the period. Keats based his poem *Lamia* (1820) on the charms of a serpent lady derived from the folklore lamia types, described by Edward Topsell in his *Historie of Four-footed Beastes* (1607), as 'poeticall alligories of beautifull Harlottes, who after they

Gustav Klimt's *Mermaids*, c.1899, disembodied sirens who haunt the ocean depths shrouded in their own hair.

have had their lust by men, doe many times devour and made them away'. A more refined but no less deadly variant, Keats' siren is the agent of her lover's death in a dramatic confrontation reminiscent of Raymond's ill-advised home-truths from *Melusine*:

> 'A serpent! echoed he; no sooner said,
> Than with a frightful scream she vanished:
> And Lycius' arms were empty of delight,
> As were his limbs of life, from that same night.

A creeping disillusion with the Church stimulated by the inexorable progress of analytical science and Darwin's disturbing evolutionary theories was evident in changed interpretations of the mermaid, now more frequently represented as the victim of society. The traditional mer-quest for a soul proved a popular literary inspiration as an allegory of society's shortcomings. Matthew Arnold's poem, *The Forsaken Merman* (1849), derived much of its poignancy from its attack on the heartlessness of organized Christianity. Margaret, the village maiden who is married to a merman abandons her mer-family to return to land and regain her soul; her unhappy mer-husband follows to plead with her but is cruelly spurned:

> But ah! She gave me never a look
> For her eyes were seal'd to the holy book.

Oscar Wilde was another writer to employ the myth as an allegory of the supremacy of 'heart' over 'soul'. His fairy story, *The Fisherman and his Soul* (1891), takes as its theme a man who loses his soul in order to win his mermaid. Each year the separated soul returns siren-like, to tempt its master back. At the third attempt it wins and both are reunited, but having lived without a heart the soul has become evil and the fisherman therefore gains a worthless soul and loses his love. Hans Andersen's *Little Mermaid* (1873), commemorated in Edvard Eriksen's famous statue in Copenhagen harbour, is probably the best-known mermaid of all in another story which revolves around a central quest for a soul. Andersen's heroine endures a state of purgatory to conceal her mer-origins and win the love of the prince, all seemingly to no avail, since he subsequently chooses another. Unlucky in love and consequently bereft of her chance of a soul through a mortal marriage, the little mermaid's prospects seem pretty bleak but her fortitude wins her a reprieve, her sufferings are sublimated to martyrdom and eventual salvation is secured.

The yearning for lost pagan worlds expressed in much nineteenth-century creative literature, also manifested itself in the art of the period and a new mermaid vogue. Here too interpretations had changed; the symbolic figure of the mermaid as Vice, familiar from Medieval art, exerted a more complex attraction in an age of declining

(Right) Hans Andersen's poignant story of a self-sacrificing mermaid's quest for love and an immortal soul, 'The Little Mermaid', has inspired many artists. This dramatic illustration of the meeting with the sea-witch is by Harry Clarke from a 1916 edition.

(Opposite) Edward Burne-Jones' *The Depths of the Sea*, 1887. A drowning youth is dragged irrevocably down by his captor. Such macabrely imaginative twists had much current appeal.

The nineteenth-century siren vogue even extended to wallpaper design. Edward Burne-Jones reworked his drawing (above) with the help of William Morris into this mermaid pattern (right), c.1880.

Christian belief. The symbolism of the Classical dream which had inspired the formal allegories of Renaissance art, fascinated nineteenth-century artists in a more personal, frequently mystical sense, and the epic Renaissance scale was increasingly narrowed in favour of the intimate drama of private tragedy. As submarine *femme fatale*, the mermaid was the perfect symbol of the attractions of doomed passion, a favourite theme frequently indulged with a masochistic thrill, as in Burne-Jones' painting, *The Depths of the Sea* (1887), which endowed its grisly subject with a haunting beauty.

John William Waterhouse's *A Mermaid*, 1900. Originally intended as a Diploma work (to be presented to the Royal Academy at the time of his election as an Academician), it was not completed until five years later.

(Opposite) Diablerie on the ocean bed: Jean Delville's
Satan's Treasure, 1895.

The image of woman as destroyer was remarkably pervasive in late nineteenth-century art. In France the Symbolists employed the theme as a controversial expression of their renunciation of established convention. The predatory siren, her hybrid form suggestive of all manner of bestial perversion, served to epitomize the Symbolist cult of decadence keenly pursued as a form of social defiance. Gustave Moreau, 'forever sorrowful, haunted by the symbols of superhuman perversities and superhuman loves', as described by J. K. Huysmans in *Against Nature* (1884), was among the many Symbolist painters inspired by the fatal enchantresses of classical myth. His elaborate nostalgic visions of antiquity dominated by cruel, inaccessible beauties are heavily inbued with the despair of unrequited desire.

Contemporary with the Symbolists and another captive to the Classical dream was the Swiss artist, Arnold Böcklin. While reflecting the prevalent obsession with the triumphant *femme fatale*, his scenes of marine myth have a boisterous Teutonic vigour quite alien to the contrived stillness of Moreau's highly detailed fantasies. Böcklin's lusty mer-folk, living out a series of orgiastic marine fantasies with

(Above) A mermaid meets her match in this Art Nouveau inkwell. (Right) Mermaid and octopus on an enamel plaque by Ernestine Evans Mills, c.1910.

Arnold Böcklin's self-portrait painted to the eerie accompaniment of Death on the violin, c.1872.

ebullient vulgarity, are a far cry from the haughty beauties of High Victorian and Symbolist art. The lurking humour disconcerted many contemporary critics, among them Claude Phillips, who cautiously remarked in the *Magazine of Art* (1885), that Böcklin:

> succeeds so thoroughly in giving form and life to the mythical beings in a sense created anew by him, that the effect produced is often a startling one – so strong is the contrast between the theme and its treatment; nay, the boundaries which separate art from the purely grotesque are often reached and well-nigh transgressed.

The Modern Mermaid

By the beginning of the twentieth century a certain humorous detachment had become increasingly evident in mermaid treatments. If the mood had changed however, the fascination still remained.

Mermaids at Play, 1886, part of a cycle of orgiastic marine fantasies painted by Arnold Böcklin in the 1880s.

Post-Freudian thought had exposed the legendary fish-tailed seductress as the personification of the hidden desires of the sexual subconscious, symbolizing primitive castration anxieties and the urge to return to the amniotic waters of the womb. Firmly characterized as an element of the unconscious, the mermaid now abandoned her marine habitat to re-emerge in the irrational dream settings of the Surrealist imagination. Magritte was one of the earliest artists to take such liberties, his stranded inverted 'mermaid' of *L'Invention Collective* (1934) neatly and humorously underlining the perverse eroticism of her original. Paul Delvaux, a later Surrealist much influenced by Magritte introduced the mermaid into his modern dream landscapes

'The Origin of the Harp', from *Thomas Moore's Irish Melodies*, illustrated by Daniel Maclise, 1845. The sea siren weeping for her lost lover is transformed into a harp.

The origin of the Harp.

'Tis believ'd that this Harp, which I wake now for thee,
Was a Siren of old, who sung under the sea;
And who often, at eve, thro' the bright waters rov'd,
To meet, on the green shore, a youth whom she lov'd.

But she lov'd him in vain, for he left her to weep,
And in tears, all the night her gold tresses to steep;
Till heav'n look'd with pity on true-love so warm,
And chang'd to this soft Harp the sea-maiden's form.

Gustave Moreau's
Galatea, c.1880. In
classical myth, Galatea
repeatedly spurned the
love of the clumsy giant
Polyphemus, who even-
tually retaliated by
crushing his more
favoured rival with
a rock.

(Opposite) J.M.W. Turner's *Glaucus and Scylla*, 1841.

in which alluring sirens beckon to oblivious passing businessmen, the contemporary stereotype of masculine frustration.

The conception of the mermaid in polite society and the humorous ramifications of that unlikely condition have become a popular twentieth-century theme. Clearly inspired by such bizarre possibilities, H. G. Wells in *The Sea Lady* (1902) wove a delightful story around the insinuation of a charming young mermaid into the middle-class Bunting household, holidaying at the English resort, Folkestone. Disquieting vistas of a life-cycle quite lacking in the correct moral propieties were opened up during her stay, as in the following tea-time conversation:

> 'What *do* you wear?' asked Miss Glendower. 'Very charming things I expect.'
> 'Its a different costume altogether,' said the Sea Lady, and brushed away a crumb. Just for a moment Mrs Bunting regarded her visitor fixedly. She had, I fancy, in that moment, an indistinct, imperfect glimpse of pagan possibilities.

Unfortunately the Sea Lady's quest for a soul centres on Miss Glendower's fiancé, the dashing Harry Chatteris. The lure of 'pagan possibilities' proves too strong and the two elope one moonlit night into the sea, leaving Cousin Melville to speculate in true Burne-Jones style on the nature of Chatteris' final end:

> Did there come a sudden horror upon him at the last, a sudden perception of infinite terror, and was he drawn down, swiftly and terribly, a bubbling repentance, into those deeps? Or was she tender and wonderful to the

Rackham's illustrated titlepage to *Undine*, 1909.

last, and did she wrap her arms about him and draw him down, down until the soft waters closed above him, down into a gentle ecstacy of death?

In *The Travel Tales of Mr Joseph Jorkens* (1931), Lord Dunsaney's endearing club character entertains fellow members with the colourful episode of his own brief marriage to a mermaid. First encountered preening herself in a tank at the Grand Hotel, Aden, it was, for Jorkens at least, a case of love at first sight, as he explained wistfully:

> I suppose every girl has her surroundings in which she look her best. Certainly, half in the water and half of her out, among those rocks that the management had had covered in seaweed of every colour and a shell or two on the white sand of the floor of the tank, she looked perfectly splendid. And I told her so.

Having abducted his siren in a bath chair Jorkens attempts to turn her into a model wife and hostess but the obstacles prove too great and one day on a beach excursion, she simply swims away.

The '40s and '50s witnessed a new mermaid craze in the arts, an escapist expression of post-war optimism. The mermaid as marine liberation symbol recurs, whether the image of sexual freedom as in Paul Delvaux' siren paintings, or political freedom as personified by

'The Aquarium has recently obtained a new attraction in the person of a good looking living mermaid', commented the *Brighton Gazette* of 17 February 1886.

Arnold Böcklin's *Sea Idyll*, 1887. A scene of domestic bliss on the high seas.

the Mermaid of Warsaw, both national emblem and symbol of the Polish resistance movement in World War II. The voluptuous sinuosities of the mermaid had established her as a favourite decorative motif in history, but the sudden proliferation of the image in this period has been ascribed by British art historian Bevis Hillier to the lyrical expression of the sea's freedom from attack. Certainly mermaids were suddenly everywhere, gliding across soup bowls, romping through cartoons, even urging the delights of Perrier Water. In 1948, the mermaid took to the cinema with *Miranda*, which

Preparing for a cold winter: Margaret Fitton's busy mermaid from the cover of the magazine *Lilliput*, August 1950.

High and dry: René Magritte's *The Forbidden World*, 1949.

Life on the ocean wave: a basking mermaid (above) from a German postcard, 1904, and (right) a sea encounter from *Lilliput*, August 1950.

starred Glynis Johns as the husky siren hooked by a local doctor out fishing, and *Mr Peabody and the Mermaid*, with Ann Blythe as the amorous mermaid who causes such social confusion at a beach resort.

The Mermaid on Stage

The advent of the screen mermaid was a late expression of a long and flourishing theatrical tradition. The Renaissance taste for spectacle and veneration for classical mythology, often centred on

Glynis Johns as a proud
mer-mother in the
British film, *Miranda*,
1948.

scenes of marine triumphs, was reflected in the many elaborately staged French court 'magnificences'. One of the more splendid of these was *Balet Comique de la Reyne* (1581), which opened in grand style on an aquatic note, with Queen Louise surrounded by her bejewelled Ladies, seated in a fountain-shaped carriage drawn by sea-horses and escorted by a grand procession of tritons and sirens. In England, twelve male water nymphs each 'desguised or dressed most strangely' in white silk and flaxen wigs, clutching armfuls of bulrushes, greeted Queen Elizabeth I on her royal progress through Norfolk and Suffolk in 1578, and caused her to 'smyle and laugh withall' (*A*

A placard showing Mary Queen of Scots as a mermaid, the contemporary symbol of prostitution, posted up in Edinburgh following Darnley's murder in 1567.

Paul Delvaux, *Siren in Full Moonlight*, 1949.

Discourse of the Queene Majestie's Entertainment in Suffolk and Norfolk: Devised by Thomas Churchyarde, Gent., 1578).

Allusions to mermaid-sirens were frequent in the Elizabethan theatre. In Shakespeare's *The Comedy of Errors* (III.ii), Antipholus of Syracuse woos his sister-in-law Luciana in the following terms:

> O, train me not, sweet mermaid, with thy note
> To drown me in thy sister's flood of tears,
> Sing, siren for thyself, and I will dote;
> Spread o'er the silver waves thy golden hairs,
> And as a bed I'll take them, and there lie;
> And in that glorious supposition think
> He gains by death that hath such means to die.
> Let Love, being light, be drowned if she sink.

The nineteenth-century folk revival encouraged the creation of a number of novel aquatic stage temptresses. The story of the ill-fated water nymph, *Undine*, was successfully transferred to ballet in 1843 under the direction of Perrot, ballet master at Her Majesty's Theatre London, where it ran for eight years. Wagner's monumental *Ring* cycle, which received its first complete performance in 1876, introduced a new submarine sisterhood, the Rhinemaidens, guardians of the Ring. The challenge posed by presenting the Rhinemaidens frolicking in their underwater habitat at the start of the opera, and

'Entry of the Sirens', an engraving from *Le Balet Comique de la Reyne*, by Balthazar de Beaujoyeulx, 1581.

'The Rhine-Maidens teasing Alberich', one of Arthur Rackham's illustrations to *The Rhinegold and The Valkyrie* by Richard Wagner, 1910.

A resident of the Mermaid's Lagoon, from the 1904 London production of *Peter Pan*.

Behind the scenes at the 1876 production of *Rheingold* at Bayreuth.

propelled forwards on a mighty wave at its conclusion have inspired some of the most imaginative effects in the production history of opera.

The Russian fairy story of a Novgorod trader's marriage to a water-king's daughter inspired one of Diaghilev's most exotic touring ballets in the early twentieth century, *Sadko*. Great care was taken to evoke the underwater atmosphere and before dancing the part of Sadko in America, Adolf Bolm was a frequent visitor to the Prince of Monaco's maritime museum where he studied fish movements. Clearly the background research paid off, the *The Times* review of the London opening on 14 November 1918, thoroughly entered into the spirit of the ballet:

> Fishiness, scaliness, greenness, wetness, underwaterness – do we dare it? – Shelleyness. Queer, finny movements, a little grotesque in detail, extraordinarily watery in the whole . . . Only in such *disjecta membra* of language can one describe the wateriness, the pulsing, throbbing, deep-sea hush of *Sadko*.

Fact or Fantasy?

At the end of Jorkens' nostalgic narrative of mermaid marriage in Lord Dunsaney's story, the sceptical Terbut remarks: 'And do you mean . . . that there really are such creatures?', to which Jorkens replies, 'Well, there was this one at any rate. Whether there are any

'Sultan and Mer-kid', one of
William Heath Robinson's
illustrations to *Bill the Minder*,
1912.

more is for Science to say. And Science one day will.' To the relief of many twentieth-century escapists, science has not yet entirely explained away the mermaid who, like the Loch Ness Monster, still lurks on the borders of credibility. As long as parts of the world's oceans remain a mystery no doubt people will continue to believe in the existence of hidden submarine beings. Reported mermaid sightings while much diminished still occur, and the remoter regions of Scotland, traditional haunt of the mer-folk, have supplied several twentieth-century eye-witness accounts testified to with much apparent sincerity.

In an attempt to rationalize such sightings, science has produced a sea mammal theory reliant on the possible confusion between the mermaid and a surfacing sea cow or a basking seal. A lively imagination would be required for such mis-identification at close range, however, particularly in the case of the two favourite sea cow contenders, the dugong and manatee. With their flipper tails and

A chance meeting between a dugong and a mermaid demonstrates the unlikelihood of mistaking one for the other.

Cubist mermaids glide through an industrial landscape in Jean Metzinger's *Mermaid in a Boat*.

(Opposite) A surprise catch: *Mermaid in the Fishmonger's* by
Pauline Ellison, 1979.

habit of suckling their young in a vertical position half out of the
water, both might conceivably be mistaken at a distance for their
more glamorous marine companion. Closer inspection however
would reveal a singularly unromantic blunt stump-like head, tiny
eyes, prominent nostrils and a huge cleft upper lip. The more
graceful seal with its eloquent eyes and considerable natural curiosity
presents a stronger case – indeed its various almost human charms
have inspired a seal mythology which often overlaps with the mermaid myth. The Phoceans, a maritime tribe in Ancient Greece,
held the seal in the highest esteem, claiming descent from the nereid
Psmathe, who turned herself into a seal in an unsuccessful attempt
to confuse the lustful Aeacus, son of Zeus. An extension of the Greek
belief that the seal's body conceals a woman, Scottish folklore boasts
its *selkies*, human seals who occasionally throw off their skins and
come ashore to dance. As with the mermaids, it was believed that
possession of their sea-going equipment would secure a devoted
spouse, and the MacCodrum clan from North Uist in the Outer
Hebrides, are among those who claim to be descended from such a
mixed marriage.

The early idea of the ocean as a cradle of monsters has generated
many legends but none quite as compelling or persistent as that of the
fish-tailed siren. The mass of accumulated stories and sightings
through history provide an eloquent expression of latent eagerness
to believe in one of the most romantic myths created. Born from the
'Mother and love of men, the sea' and embodying a sexual fantasy of
universal appeal, the mermaid is clearly too glamorous a creature to
be understood by the laws of Science alone. Forever alluring, yet
never to be possessed by a living man, her reality is embedded deep
in the collective unconscious, the magnetic focus of a ceaseless
inchoate longing to dare the wild Unknown.

Sleeping mermaids from *The Children's Tennyson* by May
Byron, illustrated by N.M. Price.

Further Reading

Bassett, Fletcher S., *Legends and Superstitions of the Sea and of Sailors* (Belford, Clarke & Co., Chicago & New York, 1885; Reprinted by Gale Research Co., Detroit, Michigan, 1971).

Bennett, Alfred Gordon, *Focus on the Unknown* (Rider & Co., London, 1953; Library Publications, New York, 1954).

Benwell, Gwen, and Waugh, Sir Arthur, *Sea Enchantress* (Hutchinson & Co., London, 1961).

Carrington, Richard, *Mermaids and Mastodons* (Chatto & Windus Ltd., London, 1957; Rinehart & Co., New York, 1957).

Dance, S. Peter, *Animal Fakes and Frauds* (Sampson Low, Maidenhead, 1976).

Druce, George., 'Some abnormal and composite forms in English church architecture', *Archaeological Journal*, LXXII (1915).

Gerhardt, Mia Irene, *Old men of the sea* (Polak & Van Gennep, Amsterdam, 1967).

Grigson, Geoffrey, *The Goddess of Love* (Constable & Co Ltd., London, 1976; Stein & Day, New York, 1977; Quartet Books, London, 1978).

Harrison, Jane, 'The myths of Odysseus and the Sirens', *Magazine of Art* (1887).

Keightley, Thomas, *The Fairy Mythology* (Bohn's Antiquarian Library, London, 1850; Reprinted (1850 ed.) AMS Press, New York; (1860 ed.) Johnson Reprint Corpn., New York; (1870 ed.) Gale Research Co., Detroit, Michigan).

Lee, Henry, *Sea Fables Explained* (International Fisheries Exhibition, London, 1883).

McCulloch, Florence, 'Mediaeval Latin and French bestiaries', *Studies in Romance Languages and Literature* (University of North Carolina, 33, 1962).

Twycross, Meg, *Mediaeval Anadyomene* (Basil Blackwell, Oxford, 1972).

Picture Credits

Aldus Archive), 39; Mansell Collection, London, 29; William Morris Gallery, Walthamstow, 68 (btm); Musée des Beaux-Arts Jules Chéret, Nice, 17; Museé Condé, Chantilly (Photo: Giraudon), 43; Museés Royaux des Beaux-Arts de Belgique, Bruxelles, 71; Museum of the City of New York, 55; National Film Archive, 83; National Monuments Record, London, 13; Nationalgalerie Staatliche Museen Preussischer Kulturbesitz, Berlin (West), 72; David O'Connor, 30 (right), 32 (top); Österreichische Galerie, Vienna, 57; Palazzo della Farnesina, Rome (Photo: Scala), 21; Palazzo Poggi, Bologna (Photo: Scala), 19; Beatrice Phillpotts, 46 (top), 67, 82 (left), 92; Piccadilly Gallery, London, 58; Private Collection, 23, 41, 70 (left), 81; Public Record Office, London (Photo: Weidenfeld Archive), 84; Patricia Reed, 30 (top); Royal Academy of Arts, London, 69; Royal Doulton Tableware Ltd, 22; Brian and Sal Shuel, 80, 82 (right); Southampton Art Gallery and Museum, 85; Staatliche Kunstsammlungen Dresden, 31; Victoria & Albert Museum, London (Photo: Angelo Hornak), 27, 68 (top); Wagner Museum, Bayreuth (Photo: Weidenfeld Archive), 88 (btm); Wallraf-Richartz-Museum, Cologne, 37; Warburg Institute, London (Photo: Weidenfeld Archive), 86; Colin White, 61; Zentralsparkasse-Bank Vienna, 65.

Index

Page references in *italic* figures refer to illustrations.